Amos Hostetter;
A Successful Speculator's
Approach to Commodities Trading
by Morris Markovitz

Commodities Corporation
September 1977

AMOS BARR HOSTETTER
27 August 1902   30 January 1977

RESOLVED, that Commodities Corporation is greatly indebted to Amos Hostetter for his assistance and kind support when the Corporation was organized and during its early years. He was generous with his time and skills in training the Company's personnel. His intelligence, strength of character and ever present sense of perspective was an inspiration to everyone associated with him. Particularly striking was his willingness, at an advanced age, to undertake the exploration of new mathematical disciplines to systematize the trading techniques he had developed in a long and successful career in the trading of commodities.

Resolution of the Board of Directors
Commodities Corporation
3 February 1977

FOREWORD

Amos Hostetter cofounded Commodities Corporation (otherwise known as CC) along with Helmut Weymar back in 1969. CC is the trading shop that produced more legendary trading talent than the Yankees have All-Stars. Alumni include: Bruce Kovner, Michael Marcus, Paul Tudor Jones, Ed Seykota and more…

Hostetter was considered the wise sage and mentor of the group. He's credited with imbuing many of these trading greats with the wisdom and knowledge they used to achieve their grand heights.

Upon his untimely death in a car accident in 1977, the directors of CC commissioned one of their traders, Morris Markovitz, to gather and record Hostetter's timeless philosophy on markets and trading. The goal was to ensure future CC traders could benefit from his invaluable teachings. The resulting work was an internal booklet titled Amos Hostetter; A Successful Speculator's Approach to Commodities Trading.

Hostetter's trading philosophy could be boiled down to the following (in Hostetter's own words):

Try to acquire every bit of fundamental information available. Read extensively.
Simultaneously, post daily charts on commodities and develop a feel for trends.
Follow the fundamentals in your trading but only if and as long as the charts do not cast a negative vote.
He regarded money management as the first priority for any serious market speculator. From Markovitz (emphasis mine):

Sound money management is crucial to successful trading. The best market analysis won't get a trader to the bottom line — consistent profits — unless he has a sound money-management policy. This is an area where Mr. Hostetter excelled.

Sometimes it is hard to draw a sharp line between trading principles and money-management principles. If I were to paraphrase a famous saying, I think it would provide an accurate summary of one of Mr. Hostetter's most important trading and money-management principles: the market, to be commanded, must be obeyed. As a trader, Mr. Hostetter was aware of his own fallibility. He tried to protect himself from errors by the trading rules he used and by trying to anticipate areas of potential surprise.

This alone, however, was not enough. If the market moved against him for a reason he did not understand, he would often exit without waiting for a trading rule to take him out: as a money manager, he knew he could not afford the luxury of a prolonged argument with the market.

Perhaps his most important money-management principles was **"Take care of your losses and the profits will take care of themselves."** This means that a trader should place strong emphasis on keeping his losses small, because two or three large losses in succession would be a crippling blow.

His risk management principle of "taking care of your losses" is similar to Howard Marks of Oaktree Capital: "if we avoid the losers, the winners will take care of themselves." This truth is the single most important law of speculation. It sounds glib, but cutting your losses and letting your winners run is the most common thread amongst all great traders. If I could travel back in time 15 years, I'd go back and beat this fact into my thick skull… and I'd be much richer today for it.

Hostetter used a multi-pronged approach to assessing markets and potential trades. It's from him that Michael Marcus likely developed the "Marcus-Trifecta" to gauge markets — looking at "technicals, fundamentals, and market tone". Here's an overview of his approach to fundamentals:

Mr. Hostetter's fundamental approach was, to use his own phrase, "broad brush." This means that he would look at the overall balance sheet and the statistics that applied to the commodity in which a trade was contemplated. Then, certain basic questions would be asked:

— Will production exceed consumption this season (a stocks build-up)? If so, then the initial premise would be bearish.

— Will consumption exceed production (a stocks draw-down)? If so, then the initial premise would be bullish.

The initial premise would then be refined by other considerations. For example: weather could destroy the current production estimate for an agricultural commodity; a change in general economic conditions could destroy the demand or consumption estimate; the high price of meat could increase demand for potatoes.; the low price of corn could increase demand for soybean meal; and so forth. The last two items are intended to illustrate the flexibility, or creativity, of Mr. Hostetter's thinking, and represent the personal style he brought to commodity analysis. He held facts in the highest regard, yet he remained constantly alert to the principle that the facts can and do change.

The key phrase is flexibility of thinking, which is the opposite of stubbornness. Mr. Hostetter knew that, whatever his fundamental analysis might show today, there was a good chance it would show something different by the time the last day of the season had arrived… In brief, Mr. Hostetter would never wed himself to a precise position on the outlook for the future; he had often enough experienced the phenomenon of a significant price change before the reasons behind it became general knowledge. He kept himself prepared for surprises, in both directions, in advance. If one does a little "dreaming" about the possibilities on both sides, then he is in possession of possible explanations for surprises, and will be less hesitant to act if and when they come.

Maintaining an open-mind and staying aware of your biases is critical. Markets serve ample helpings of humble pie to those who arrogantly wed themselves to a "market prediction".

Hostetter took a nuanced approach to using technicals, similar to how we utilize price action in our trade analysis at Macro Ops. Markovitz writes:

Mr. Hostetter definitely did not accept the clear-cut dichotomy between fundamental and technical trading. Both methods can be used successfully, but he blended the two. It is my impression that Mr. Hostetter would have agreed with the following statement:

The pure fundamentalist concerns himself with production, consumption, stocks, and other basic economic data, viewing these as the causes and price as the effect, while the pure technician regards price as its own cause. In fact, to draw a sharp line of choice between these two approaches is not the best policy. Price itself should also be regarded as a fundamental. It can play the role of cause or effect or both under different circumstances.

The market's own behavior can, in a real sense, be classified as a fundamental variable. The method of analysis, however, is completely different. The technical aspect of Mr. Hostetter's trading consists primarily of:

1. Trend following
2. Support and resistance areas
3. Pattern recognition

These are listed in order of their importance, although any one of them may be the dominant influence at a given time.

Within this technical framework Hostetter employed a number of useful heuristics to help him read the tape:

Many of the techniques Mr. Hostetter used depended on a time factor. In general, as with congestion areas, most patterns accrue more significance if they take more time to form, and a trader should be aware of time as well as price when considering any technical pattern. For example, a bear market that has persisted for a year is unlikely to form its bottom in a week, nor is a two-month bull market likely to take a year to form a top. A trader should keep in mind the duration of recent major moves and expect commensurate time periods for the formation of the current pattern. (Patience is an important virtue — hastiness rarely pays).

I find Hostetter's thoughts on the "time factor" useful in analyzing where price may be headed. Markets tend to follow a certain symmetry over long periods of time. Some technical heuristics Hostetter used are:

He would become seriously concerned if a bull market was unable to make a new high for thirty days (the same is true for a bear market that hadn't made new lows for thirty days).
A poor price response to bullish news is itself an ill omen for long positions, especially if other cautionary signs are present (e.g., the bull market is old, the vigor has shown some signs of waning, prices are near a fundamental objective, etc.)
The most important timing issue is patience. One should wait for his opportunity, wait until everything lines up according to his expectations. It is far better to miss an opportunity here or there than to jump in too early without a clear plan. Too much patience is rarely the problem for any trader.
A trader should do his fundamental homework, keep his eye on the charts, and patiently observe. Once he is able to form a definite fundamental opinion, he should wait for confirming market action before proceeding.
Practicing the necessary patience to win is one of the hardest aspects of speculation. Fear is man's strongest emotion and is behind one of a trader's most common foibles — the fear of missing out (FOMO). Success comes to those who realize that Pareto's Law dominates the distribution of returns. Only a handful of trades a year will account for the majority of profits. It pays to sit and wait patiently for those fat pitches to come along.

Lastly, here's a list of maxims and trading do's and don'ts as recorded by Hostetter in his own words.

GENERAL PRINCIPLES AND MARKET MAXIMS

A very general and important rule is: take care of your losses and your profits will take care of themselves. This is both a trading maxim and a money-management tool. A trader needs big winners to pay for his losses and he won't capture these big wins unless he stays with the trend all the way.

There is never any objection to taking a loss. There must always be a good reason before you can permit yourself to close out a profit.

When in doubt, get out. Don't gamble. Be sure, however, that your doubt is based on something real (fundamentals, market action, etc.), and not simply on your own nervousness about the price level. If it is only the price level that is making you nervous, then either stick with the winner or at worst use a more sensitive stop-loss point. Give the major trend all the chance you can to increase your profits.

All major trends take a long time to work themselves out. There are times when the best approach is just to sit and do nothing, letting the power of the underlying trend work for you while others argue about the day-to-day news. Be patient.

Surprising price response to news is one of the most reliable price forecasters. Bullish response to bear news, or vice-versa, means that the price had already discounted the news and the next move will probably go the other way. Actually, this is only one example of a wider principle: When a market doesn't do what it "should", then it will probably do what it "shouldn't", and fairly soon. (Note that false breakouts, up or down, are also subsumed under this more general principle. When new lows are achieved in a long-term bear market, for example, the market ' 'should" follow through with weakness—after all, it is a bear market. If, instead, it rallies quickly, this provides some evidence against the bear market premise).

THE DANGERS IN TRADING CAUSED BY HUMAN NATURE

Fear — fearful of profit and one acts too soon.
Hope — hope for a change [in the] forces against one.
Lack of confidence in one's own judgment.
Never cease to do your own thinking.
A man must not swear eternal allegiance to either the bear or bull side. His concern lies in being right.

Laziness prevents a trader from keeping posted to the minute.
The individual fails to stick to facts.
People believe what it pleases them to believe.
DON'TS

Don't sacrifice your position for fluctuations.
Don't expect the market to end in a blaze of glory. Look out for warnings.
Don't expect the tape to be a lecturer. It's enough to see that something is wrong.
Never try to sell at the top. It isn't wise. Sell after a reaction if there is no rally.
Don't imagine that a [market] that has once sold at 150 must be cheap at 130.
Don't buck the market trend.
Don't look for breaks. Look out for warnings.
Don't try to make an average from a losing game.
Never keep goods that show a loss and sell those that show a profit. Get out with the least loss and sit tight for greater profits.

SUGGESTIONS

Experience must teach. Follow it invariably.
Observation gives the best tips of all. Observe [market] behavior and experience shows how to profit.
Buying on a rising market is the comfortable way. The point is not so much to buy as cheap as possible or go short at top prices, but to buy and sell at the right time.
Remember [a market is] never too high for you to begin buying or too low to begin selling. Let your tape reading show you when to begin. After the initial transaction don't make a second unless the first shows a profit.
There is a great deal in starting right in every enterprise.
When something happens on which you did not count when your plans were made, it behooves you to utilize the opportunity.
In a bear market it is always wise to cover if complete demoralization develops suddenly.

Stick to facts only and govern your actions accordingly.
What is abnormal is seldom a desirable factor in a trader's calculations. If a [market] doesn't act right, don't touch it.

Tips from the Great Trend Trader Amos Hostetter Jr.

Never keep goods that show a loss, and sell those that show a profit. Get out with the least loss, and sit tight for greater profits.

Never cease to do your own thinking.

A man must not swear eternal allegiance to either the bear or bull side.

The individual fails to stick to facts!

People believe what it pleases them to believe.

Amos Hostetter

Amos Hostetter;
A Successful Speculator's
Approach to Commodities Trading
by Morris Markovitz

Commodities Corporation
September 1977

Contents

Introduction

Amos Hostetter contributed to the operations of Commodities Cor-poration in a number of important ways. His trading was quite profita-ble for the firm. More important, his strength of character, humanity and intelligence were a source of inspiration to all of his colleagues and proteges. He contributed enthusiastically to the education and training of much of today's Commodities Corporation management, and was personally responsible for the hiring of some members of that management.

For these reasons and others, the management and Directors of Com-modities Corporation decided in the Fall of 1976 to recognize Mr. Hostetter's contributions by dedicating our new facilities to him. We subsequently commissioned the portrait by Peter Cook which serves as the frontispiece to this booklet and now hangs in our lobby.

After his untimely death in an automobile accident in January 1977, we felt that we should document the basic elements of Mr. Hostetter's trading approach while these were still fresh in our minds. He was the consummate trader. He was disciplined, intelligent, and informed. He never lost his perspective. Happily, he was also articulate, and in various letters and memoranda he committed to writing his views on the proper approach to trading. Further, he enjoyed the give and take involved in discussing these views with his younger colleagues. So we were fortunate in having a firm foundation for the preparation of this booklet.

Morry Markovitz was the natural choice to take on the documentation task. Morry is a trader, and was close to Mr. Hostetter. As part of Morry's training process, the two spent many hours discussing trading techniques. To help fix Mr. Hostetter's trading views in his own mind, Morry had already written a summary of those views some time ago.

Amos Hostetter's approach to trading was timeless. We hope that with this booklet we will in a sense extend through time his constant willingness to share that approach with others.

F. Helmut Weymar
September 15, 1977

I. Mr. Hostetter's Trading Philosophy

What follows is an attempt to describe the general trading philosophy that made Mr. Hostetter a great speculator. Of necessity, it cannot be a complete description. Only Amos himself could have supplied that, and even then the reader would have had to contend with the great gulf between the description of a philosophy and the actual living of it. However, Amos was always generous with his knowledge and his ideas. He left us with volumes of material, in his own written work and in the memories of those who knew him. Perhaps the briefest summary of his trading philosophy is, in his own words, the following:

> "1. Try to acquire every bit of fundamental information available. Read extensively.
>
> 2. Simultaneously, post daily charts on commodities and develop a feel for trends.
>
> Follow the fundamentals in your trading but only *if* and *as long as* the charts do not cast a negative vote."
>
> (January 23, 1975)

In the pages which follow, details will expand on this bare outline. They will be details of fact and of method. The method is more important than the particulars — specific markets change, the economic environment changes. The future may invalidate many of the particulars we rely upon today. It is therefore important to know the fundamental axioms that will always apply and to have a method or approach that is simultaneously logical, fact-oriented, and yet flexible enough not merely to meet with change, but to embrace it and capital-ize on it. This is what Mr. Hostetter was able to accomplish in a field where success stories are very rare.

Before going further, the reader may wish to glance at Appendix A entitled "Some Observations on Trading in Commodity Futures." This is a brief piece written by Mr. Hostetter in April of 1966, containing a checklist of questions a trader should ask himself during the initiation, maintenance, and close-out of a trading position.

We now turn to the philosophy itself, which consists of proper money-management and both a fundamental and a technical approach to trading. A good part of it will not come as news to one who is well acquainted with trading. One of the keys to Mr. Hostetter's success, aside from his own creativity, was his ability to grasp the oft-repeated but so frequently misunderstood or mis-applied truisms of trading. In other words, he was able to complete the job of actually living and acting by his philosophy: He turned platitudes into dollars. This is perhaps the most difficult step for a trader, and Mr. Hostetter was justly proud, in his own quiet way, of his success "at the bottom line." The reader is therefore reminded that what follows is not an automatic key to successful trading. Although there is a great deal to be mined from Mr. Hostetter's philosophy, that final step to the bottom line is by a route that each trader must find for himself.

II Money Management

Sound money management is crucial to successful trading. The best market analysis won't get a trader to the bottom line consistent profits unless he has a sound money- management policy. This is an area where Mr. Hostetter excelled.

Sometimes it is hard to draw a sharp line between trading principles and money-management principles. If I were to paraphrase a famous saying, I think it would provide an accurate summary of one of Mr. Hostetter's most important trading and money-management princi-ples: the market, to be commanded, must be obeyed. As a trader, Mr. Hostetter was aware of his own fallibility. He tried to protect himself from errors by the trading rules he used and by trying to anticipate areas of potential surprise. This alone, however, was not enough. If the market moved against him for a reason he did not understand, he would often exit without waiting for a trading rule to take him out: as a money-manager, he knew he could not afford the luxury of a prolonged argument with the market.

Perhaps his most important money-management principle was "Take care of your losses and the profits will take care of themselves." This means that a trader should place strong emphasis on keeping his losses small, because two or three large losses in succession would be a crippling blow. Such a blow is inevitable for the trader who takes large risks frequently. Mr. Hostetter would adjust the size of his position according to both the risk/reward ratio and the absolute risk in dollars, keeping his exposure to losses relatively small. The questionnaire in Appendix A vetoes any trade if it risks more than 25 percent of one's total commodity funds. Mr. Hostetter was actually even more strin-gent in his trading: I think it was a quite rare occurrence for him to risk as much as 10 percent of his equity on any single trading idea.

With regard to position size, there was sometimes another ingredient in the decision - making process: Mr. Hostetter seemed to be influ-enced by his own recent performance. After a period of setbacks, he would voluntarily scale down the level of his operations. There were times (not often, but there were times) when he would go for as long as several weeks with nothing larger than token positions. Sometimes this may have resulted from the lack of opportunities. But I am certain that there were times when it was due to disappointment with his own recent performance.

This must have taken a great deal of self-awareness and self-discipline. It was, perhaps, an instance of refusing to blame the market for his own lack of good results, of facing an unpleasant fact and acting ac-cordingly because it was, after all, a fact. This must also have taken a great deal of self-confidence — the confidence to wait, trusting all the while in his eventual return to full-scale operations.

III The Fundamental Approach

Mr. Hostetter's fundamental approach was, to use his own phrase, "broad brush." This means that he would look at the overall balance sheet and the statistics that applied to the commodity in which a trade was contemplated. Then, certain basic questions would be asked:

— Will production exceed consumption this season (a stocks build-up)? If so, then the initial premise would be bearish.
— Will consumption exceed production (a stocks draw-down)? If so, then the initial premise would be bullish.

The initial premise would then be refined by other considerations. For example: weather could destroy the current production estimate for an agricultural commodity; a change in general economic conditions could destroy the demand or consumption estimate; the high price of meat could increase demand for potatoes; the low price of corn could increase demand for soybean meal; and so forth. The last two items are intended to illustrate the flexibility, or creativity, of Mr. Hostetter's thinking, and represent the personal style he brought to commodity analysis. He held facts in the highest regard, yet he remained constantly alert to the principle that the facts can and do change.

The key phrase is *flexibility of thinking,* which is the opposite of stubbornness. Mr. Hostetter knew that, whatever his fundamental analysis might show today, there was a good chance it would show something different by the time the last day of the season had arrived. So he would try to anticipate the general areas from which changes could come, using the facts at hand (e.g., current and anticipated conditions in related markets) as clues to guide him to the areas of potential surprise. In brief, Mr. Hostetter would never wed himself to a precise position on the outlook for the future; he had often enough experienced the phenomenon of a significant price change before the reasons behind it became general knowledge. He kept himself pre-pared for surprises, in both directions, in advance. If one does a little "dreaming" about the possibilities on both sides, then he is in posses-sion of possible explanations for surprises, and will be less hesitant to act if and when they come.

This is not to imply that Mr. Hostetter was merely a "dreamer." He had a fertile imagination, but the facts came first. He wasn't satisfied with a good idea until he saw evidence to support it. He was quantita-tive and liked to see correlations of fundamental factors or fundamen-tal indices with price; scatter diagrams, long-range trends of supply/demand statistics; and so on. He did like to keep his basic set of fundamental tools as simple as possible, although he was always eager to consider new ideas. He was never concerned with extremely precise knowledge of a market. He used the "broad brush", and he wanted to see whatever could be successfully related to price.

There are two examples of what Mr. Hostetter would have called "broad brush" analysis in Appendix B. One is a forecast of the 1972/1973 bull market in soybeans, and the other is a set of graphs of production and stocks that Mr. Hostetter used to analyze the potato market. It cannot be overemphasized that "broad brush" does *not* mean vague. It means a clear view of the current general situation and an open mind about possible changes.

IV The Technical Approach

The justification of the technical approach is partially given in the preceding section: the price itself often reflects important factors which are not yet generally known. This is the standard justification of technical trading, namely that all factors will be visible in the price and that price alone is therefore sufficient to forecast itself. Mr. Hostetter didn't fully accept this last statement; otherwise he wouldn't have bothered to look at fundamentals. However, the market does consist of people making decisions, and patterns do emerge. Some of these are reliable enough to justify a position even without much knowl-edge of the fundamentals (although Mr. Hostetter would quickly check into the fundamentals if such a pattern did emerge).

Mr. Hostetter definitely did not accept the clear-cut dichotomy be-tween fundamental and technical trading. Both methods can be used successfully, but he blended the two. It is my impression that Mr. Hostetter would have agreed with the following statement:

The pure fundamentalist concerns himself with production, con-sumption, stocks, and other basic economic data, viewing these as the causes and price as the effect, while the pure technician re-gards price as its own cause. In fact, to draw a sharp line of choice between these two approaches is not the best policy. Price itself should also be regarded as a fundamental. It can play the role of cause or effect or both under different circumstances.

The market's own behavior can, in a real sense, be classifiable as a fundamental variable. The method of analysis, however, is completely different. The technical aspect of Mr. Hostetter's trading consists primarily of:

1. trend following
2. support and resistance areas
3. pattern recognition

These are listed in order of their importance, although any one of them may be the dominant influence at a given time. In addition to these three factors, Mr. Hostetter developed several specialized rules and techniques that can apply under certain circumstances.

Mr. Hostetter developed a computerized version of some of his technical methods. It has been successful (the system has proven itself with profits) but not as successful as Mr. Hostetter's own trading. This system will be discussed in more detail in Section V.

Basic Technical Approach

Trend Following

One should always hold in his mind the direction of the major, intermediate, and short-term trends. The major trend is the most powerful. Trade with the trend, and you will be right more often than you are wrong.

A bull market is a major uptrend, and a bear market is a major downtrend. In most commodities, the time involved in a major trend is usually at least three or four months. (A trend can also be sideways. If so, it is usually best to regard the immediately preceding trend as still in force until proven otherwise or until there is some non-technical reason for believing otherwise.)

If we look at the intermediate high and low points that comprise a major trend, then:

A bull (bear) market is a sequence of successively higher (lower) highs and successively higher (lower) lows.

When this criterion is violated, a warning flag goes up: the major trend may be about to change. The diagram of a bear market raising this flag is shown below, with the first warning given in one of two ways:

FIGURE 1
Two warning signals of a possible trend reversal in a bear market.

1. A higher high

2. A higher low

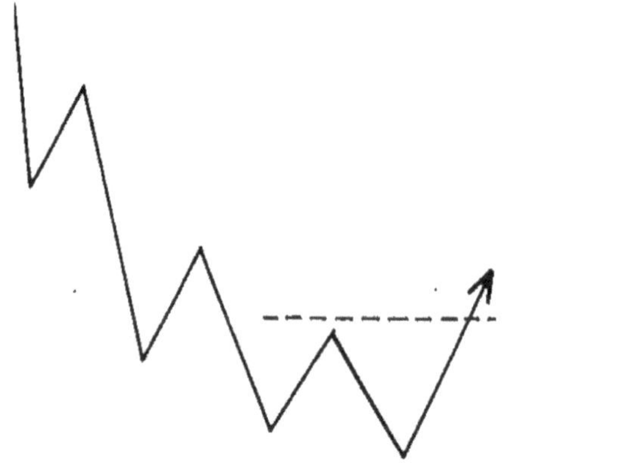

The genuine warning is Case 1, because a new high has been made. Case 2, however, does arouse suspicion, and *might* induce one to cover short positions, especially if other factors support that action. Case 2 will turn into a Case 1 if and when the immediately prior high point is exceeded.

Once this occurs, it is definitely time to cover short positions, and to think about establishing longs. One should buy immediately or else wait for the first pullback, depending on how strong the bullish merits appear (the fundamentals and the risk versus the potential reward). If the price pulls back and steadies again before reaching its prior low point, the market can be bought with stop-loss orders under that prior low; at least a partial position may be taken. Subsequent confirmation of the trend reversal (a new penetration above the prior high) means that the balance of a full long position can be taken. In the meanwhile, one should be watching for other signs of a bottoming formation (see *Pattern Recognition* section below).

It should be remembered that all major trends have reactions against the trend. These are usually (but not always) swifter than the prior move with the trend. Sharp reactions in bull markets and sharp rallies in bear markets are par for the course and provide a little more evidence that the major trend is intact. A slowly halting advance in an uptrend, weakening and starting to give ground, provides more of an indication that the trend will turn down than a swift collapse. The converse is true for bear markets. In general, the greater the time spent in a narrow range, subsequent to a major move, the greater is the likelihood that the trend will reverse.

One should never underestimate the power of a major trend. This principle may be repeated in some of the following sections, because Mr. Hostetter regarded it as crucial.

Support and Resistance Areas
Support and resistance are very important clues to the direction of price. Support and resistance are two different terms to describe a

18

congestion area on a price chart. A congestion area is a fairly well defined, or bounded, price area within which the market has stagnated for some time before making a clear move one way or the other. When prices return toward such a previous congestion area from above, that area may provide support for the decline. When prices move upward toward a congestion area, that area may provide resistance to the advance.

If, upon first approach, prices slice well into such an area (more than half way), then most likely the ultimate resolution will be to carry prices through and beyond that area, even if a bit of pull-back or congestion occurs first. If, on the other hand, prices halt, begin to congest, or turn back before they enter the area (less than half way), then it is most likely that the support or resistance area will hold.

In the two illustrations below, the next move will probably be upward.

FIGURE 2

The next move is likely to be higher, because congestion is taking place in the *upper* part of the price range of the prior congestion area.

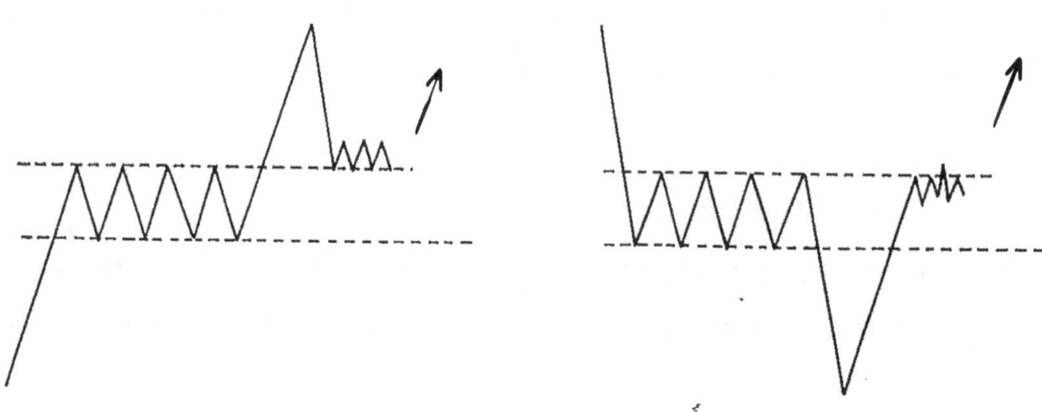

In the two illustrations below, the next move will probably be downward.

FIGURE 3

The next move is likely to be lower because congestion is taking place in the *lower* part of the price range of the prior congestion area.

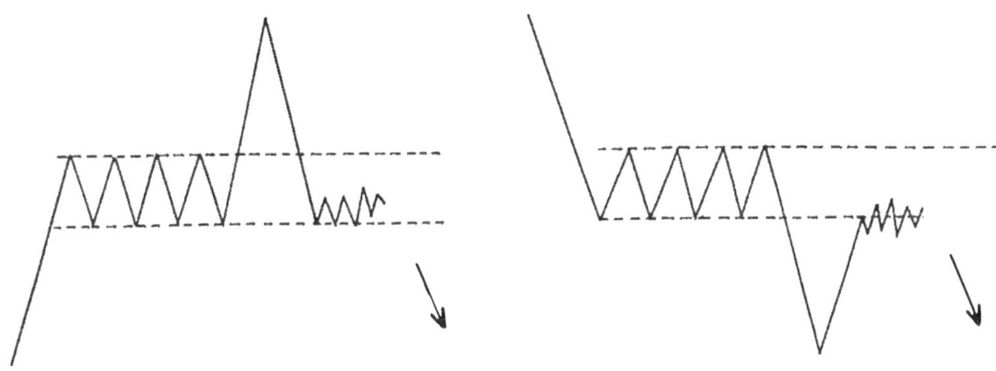

In summary, the more a support/resistance area is penetrated upon first approach, the more likely it is to yield. The less it is penetrated, the less likely it is to yield.

Finally, a greater time spent in forming a support/resistance area gives that area greater significance.

Pattern Recognition

Pattern recognition is a broad subject. Its validity is based on the premise that certain visual patterns exhibited by price are not random, but rather are the effects of underlying causes. From similar patterns one can infer the operation of similar underlying causes and project the future course of price. Support and resistance areas, discussed above, are only one subset of a variety of recognizable patterns.

Books have been written about recognizing patterns on price charts. This form of technical analysis ascribes importance to chart patterns that look like triangles, pennants, diamonds, flags, channels, etc. Al-though this particular type of pattern recognition has some value, Mr. Hostetter considered support/resistance to be the most important visual patterns.

Mr. Hostetter was, however, a strong believer in the validity of certain kinds of patterns under certain circumstances. Patterns on past charts that were similar to a current pattern *in the same market* were consid-ered to be of definite value, and not merely random. This was es-pecially true if the patterns were formed under external conditions that were known to have been similar. If the fundamental situations in the past were similar, for example, then a similar price pattern could be an important clue to the current situation.

Some patterns give clues to a possible reversal in the major trend. A classic bottoming pattern consists of a generally sideways movement, often in an ever-narrowing price range, and often on a low and de-creasing volume of trading. Sometimes the price pattern will narrow almost to a point before the upmove begins. If these patterns are also present when the warning signal depicted in Figure 1 occurs, then a long position can be taken with greater confidence (more ag-gressively). Mr. Hostetter liked to buy under these circumstances because they offered low risk. If the fundamental outlook left room for a potential bull market, then he might have become enthusiastic about a long position under these conditions,even before the major trend reversal was confirmed. The more of the bottoming criteria present, and the better the risk/reward ratio, the more enthusiastic he would be. (It should be noted that, while the above bottoming criteria apply to most commodities, they do not apply to all. Some com-modities have their own distinct peculiarities. Pork Bellies, for exam-ple, are notorious for their "spike" bottoms.)

With tops, the problem is more difficult. The warning flag of Figure 1 is always an extremely important sign and is usually sufficient to jus-tify liquidation of long and initiation of short positions. Because tops are more complex than bottoms, they will be discussed in the follow-ing section, on Mr. Hostetter's
Other Technical Methods.

One last consideration that properly falls under the *Pattern Recognition* category is time. Many of the techniques Mr. Hostetter used de-pended on a time factor. In general, as with congestion areas, most patterns accrue more significance if they take more time to form, and a trader should be aware of time as well as price when considering any technical pattern. For example, a bear market that has persisted for a year is unlikely to form its bottom in a week, nor is a two-month bull market likely to take a year to form a top. A trader should keep in mind the duration of recent major moves and expect commensurate time periods for the formation of the current pattern. (Patience is an important virtue—hastiness rarely pays).

Other Technical Methods

Market Tops

One of the more difficult tasks for both the fundamentalist and the technician is top-picking. Tops in most commodity markets are often wild and volatile. Although Mr. Hostetter would occasionally pick bottoms on the basis of his fundamental know ledge, he would rarely do so with tops. Rather, he would prefer to let the market speak for itself; i.e., he would place very heavy emphasis on market action as the best means for indicating a top.

Tops are formed, obviously, subsequent to the uptrend of a bull mar-ket. It is usually a mistake to pick a top on the basis of the price level alone. (Don't abandon the major trend unless you have very good reasons!)

Some tops are broad, some are "spike" tops, and some are difficult to describe with a single word. In brief, tops are complex and varied, so a trader needs to learn their many different signs.

One method has already been mentioned, the warning flag of Figure 1. A decline that carries prices below the immediately prior intermediate low usually means that long positions should be jettisoned.

Sometimes, the immediately prior low point is so far below current prices that the above rule would result in losing most of the existing profit. This is the case when a market makes a fairly straight advance for a great distance without interruption. Mr. Hostetter's exit from

this or other difficult tops could occur for any of several possible reasons, depending on the market's behavior:

A) The market may have a reaction, rally, and fall back even lower, activating the rule already mentioned above.

B) In the meanwhile, Mr. Hostetter would retain, as a kind of last resort, a mental stop-loss point: should a reaction exceed 60 percent of the distance (price-wise) of the immediately prior upmove, he would liquidate longs. In practice, Mr. Hostetter rarely had to resort to this safety net in order to preserve his profits. Most often some other criterion would be satisfied first. However, the safety net was always there as a money-management tool, to prevent disaster.

This 60-percent rule must be carefully applied, as is illustrated in Fugure 4.

FIGURE 4
The 60% Rule.

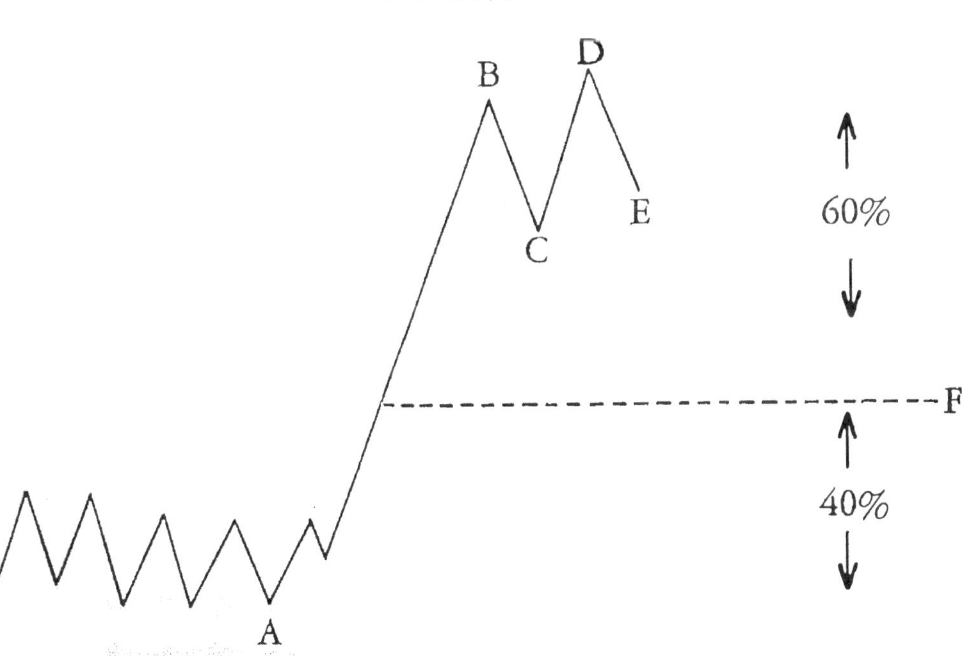

The 60% rule is used as a last resort or safety net to avoid giving back all profits in the rare cases when one of the other top-picking rules is not triggered. It is important to remember that this rule applies only in the context of the major trend. The move from A to D is a major leg, or wave, of a bull market, and F marks the level of a 60% retracement. Should prices reach as low as F before any other rules are triggered, Mr. Hostetter would have exited from long positions. Note that the decline from D to E does *not* trigger the 60% rule. The rule is not intended to be applied in congestion areas or against intermediate or minor moves, such as the minor advance from C to D.

C) Mr. Hostetter would become seriously concerned if a bull market was unable to make a new high for thirty days (the same is true for a bear market that hadn't made new lows for thirty days). He might also have become concerned if his fundamental price objective had been reached, and especially so if the market's vigor (ability to rally strongly) seemed to be waning at the same time. If either or both of these situations obtained, Mr. Hostetter still would not try to pick a top. However, he would become very sensitive to the market action, by using a six-day rule: if prices decline to lower than the lowest point of the preceding six days, he would sell, and possibly sell short, depending on his general view of the market and the risk/reward.

D) A false breakout might have caused Mr. Hostetter to sell. A false breakout is described in more detail later, but it is basically the following:

After congesting for a while near their highs, prices then break out upward to new high ground. However, there is no follow-through — i.e., the price quickly retreats well back into the prior congestion area (see *Support and Resistance Areas* section). This lack of strength usually implies impending weakness, especially if it occurs on bullish news.

E) A poor price response to bullish news is itself an ill omen for long positions, especially if other cautionary signs are present (e.g., the bull market is old, the vigor has shown some signs of waning, prices are near a fundamental objective, etc.).

Depending on the bullishness of the news, the degree of the market's poor response, and the number and quality of other cautionary signs, Mr. Hostetter would have either exited immediately or resorted to his six-day rule.

F) If a straight and uninterrupted upmove is followed by a steep but major reaction that approaches or exceeds 50 percent of the prior move, after which the uptrend resumes, then none of the above rules will have been triggered, not even the 60 percent rule. However, a reaction of this magnitude is worrisome and the subsequent rally bears watching. The market's high point (H) and the reaction low point (L) are the measuring points. On the basis of these, a judgment must be made about the current rally, as to whether it is a new leg in the existing bull market or the first rally in a newly forming bear market. This judgment depends on how far the rally carries before it starts to hesitate or congest.

Specifically if prices return more than halfway from L to H and congest in the top half of the area between L and H, then the bull market is probably intact. If they return less than halfway, and/or congestion is predominantly in the bottom half, then one should probably sell out (see Figure 5).

FIGURE 5
After a substantial price decline in a bull market (see text)

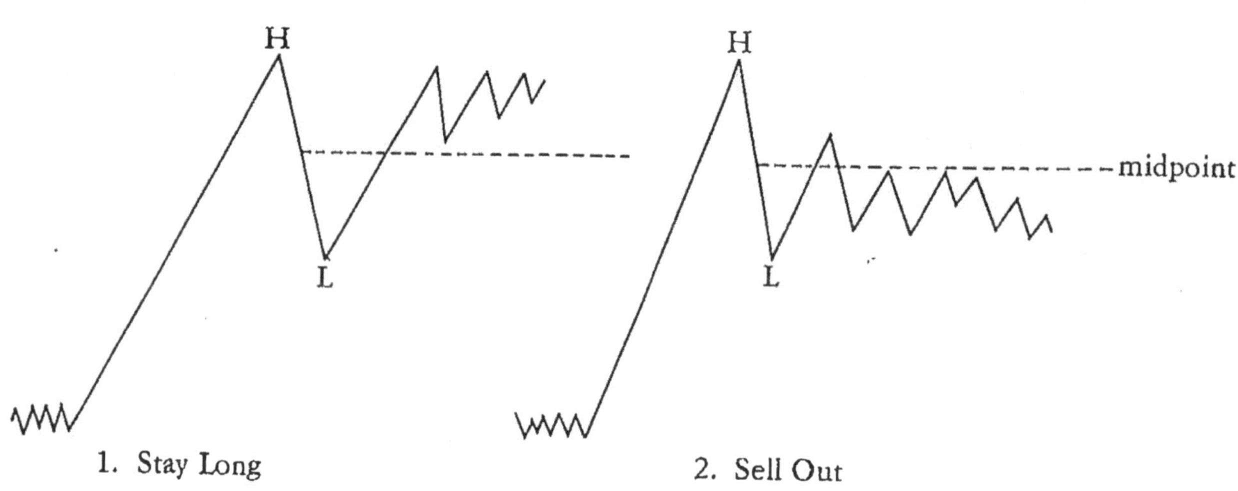

G) The "right shoulder" should be sold. If, after some (but not conclusive) topping signs, a market has a sharp enough break to indicate strongly the beginning of a bear market, then the next rally should be sold short. This is really a version of rule F under circumstances when Mr. Hostetter had been anticipating a possible end to the bull market for standard fundamental or other reasons. With strong enough reasons in hand, he would immediately adopt a bear market premise upon the sharp decline, and look eagerly for a spot to sell on the subsequent rally, with stop-loss orders initially entered over contract highs.

Patience, Timing and Special Techniques

A) Perhaps the most important timing issue is patience. One should wait for his opportunity, wait until everything lines up according to his expectations. It is far better to miss an opportunity here or there than to jump in too early without a clear plan. Too much patience is rarely the problem for any trader.

A trader should do his fundamental homework, keep his eye on the charts, and patiently observe. Once he is able to form a definite fundame`al opinion, he should wait for confirming market action befo`e roceeding.

B) The thirty-day rule mentioned in the preceding section gives an idea of the time scales in which Mr. Hostetter thought. In the absence of strong countervailing evidence, he would sometimes hold a position for as long as thirty days beyond new highs or new lows before getting nervous. "The big money is made in the big moves", and Mr. Hostetter was able to stick with his positions long enough to take full advantage of this truism. (See Appendix C).

C) The six-day rule mentioned earlier was arrived at by a study of many market tops. A five-day rule gave many false signals and a seven-day rule was not significantly more reliable than the six-day. When a bull market looks suspicious enough to make one nervous, the six-day rule should be used. The reason Mr. Hostetter chose this type of strategy is that he was a firm believer in the power of the major trend—of its tendency to persist. Thus, despite his own suspicions, he would still grant the trend at least one last chance to prove itself before abandoning his position. The six-day rule showed itself to be a serviceable tool in this regard.

D) Time is also a factor in false breakouts that occur in either direction. The false breakout was briefly described in the *Top-Picking* section. Mr. Hostetter would usually sell after false upward moves only if the market was at a high price level relative to the recent past (three to twelve months). Similarly, he would prefer not to buy after false downward breaks unless the price level was low. Consider Figure 6:

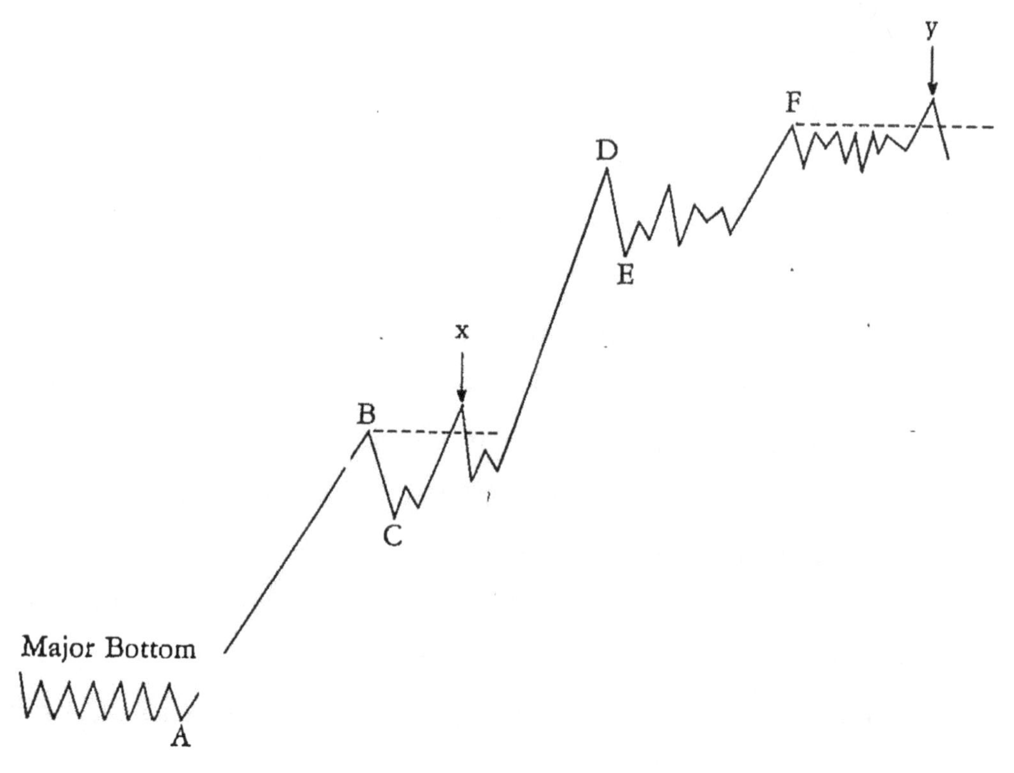

FIGURE 6
The False Breakout (see text)

The arrow at y marks a false upward breakout. This particular bull move had three major waves or legs: from A to B, then from C to D, then from E to F. Note that the third major advance did not carry very far into new high ground. Although not conclusive, it does raise the possibility that the bull trend is losing steam. The extended congestion area after F was followed by a move toward or into new highs (arrow at y), which confirmed the uptrend at the time it happened. However, almost immediately afterward the market retreated well back into the previous congestion area. The suspicions about the market's loss of vigor are considered to be confirmed. Hence longs should be liquidated, because the bull market may well be over; even if it isn't, chances favor a period of prolonged and/or extensive weakness. Enough doubt has been raised to undermine the justification for a long position.

By way of comparison, it should be noted that the decline after x was *not* a false breakout. For one thing, it occurred too early in the move to raise major doubts. For another, it did not fall well back into the prior congestion. Finally, the congestion itself was too brief.

E) If a major trend is underway, and one does not have a position, then it will often pay to take a position on the first reaction that retraces 45 percent or so of the initial move, if that reaction comes swiftly. This is true in the early stages of what appears to be a new major trend. Losses can then be limited by the 60-percent rule. (Of course, a 45-percent reaction may never occur, in which case one will miss the move. Also, if we are concerned with the sale of the first bear market rally, a 65-percent stop may be used instead, to allow for the greater volatility of tops).

F) Intermediate highs and lows are visually apparent on price charts, for the most part. These are the points that define the trend. As long as each reaction does not carry past the previous one, the major trend is considered intact. Even though these points are usually obvious on the charts, there are two special circumstances that also qualify as reactions:

i) Any move that carries prices back more than 5 percent of the absolute price level from its extreme point (high or low) may be regarded as a bona fide reaction once the trend resumes (new highs or new lows), and stops can then be placed accordingly.

ii) In a major trend, it is rare for prices to close against the trend more than two or three days in succession. Thus, if one is on the sidelines of a bear market, a two- or three-day rally is usually a selling opportunity. If the market were to rally four days in a row, however (closing basis), this is a strong cautionary sign. If five days in a row, then the move may be regarded as a bona fide reaction regardless of its extent.

FIGURE 7
Five successive counter-trend daily closings constitute a bona-fide
intermediate reaction.

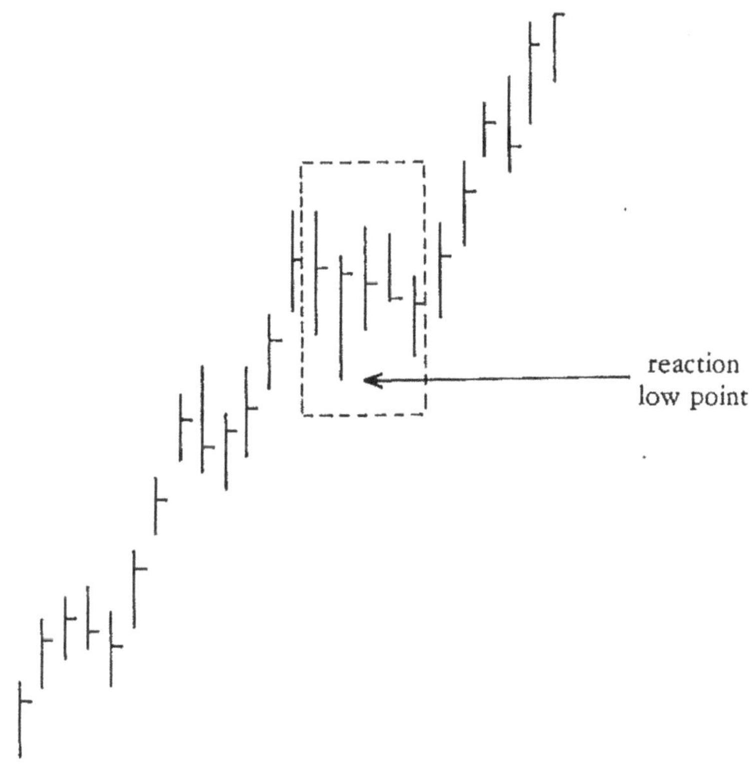

There were five successively lower closing prices during an
uptrend, as shown in the dotted box of Figure 7. The total
decline may have been less than 1 percent of the price
level, but the five-in-a-row decline is significant. If and
when the trend resumes upward, then the low point of the
activity within the box may be regarded as a bona fide
reaction low, and stops placed beneath it (arrow).

V Mr. Hostetter's Computerized Trading System

Over the course of the past several years, working with Commodities Corporation's computer department, Mr. Hostetter developed a computerized trading program that automatized many of his trading techniques.

It is a testament to Mr. Hostetter's active and energetic mind that he undertook to learn computer programming language while in his 70's, in order to facilitate his communication with the programmers. He devoted a great deal of time and energy to this program, working in the evenings and weekends, poring over the computer printouts, plotting the simulated transactions, and attempting to include more of his own methods and to ensure that they were accurately encoded. He was still actively involved in all these efforts at the time of his death.

Although research was constantly being done to improve the program, a current version has been trading real funds since 1974, and trading them profitably. The program uses purely technical criteria for decision-making, such as high and low points, time, and special pattern recognition. It is not a typical trend-following system, although it is virtually impossible for the program to miss a major trend.

The development of the program provided evidence of the degree of generality of Mr. Hostetter's trading techniques. The parameters were originally derived from simulations on only two commodities, yet these identical parameters later proved to be successful for trading a large number of other commodities.

VI Some General Principles and Market Maxims

A) A very general and important rule is: *take care of your losses and your profits will take care of themselves.* Appendix A makes this point strongly. It means that Mr. Hostetter's approach is to make it easy to abandon losing positions and difficult to exit from winners. This is both a trading maxim and a money-management tool. A trader needs big winners to pay for his losses and he won't capture these big wins unless he stays with the trend all the way.

There is never any objection to taking a loss. There must always be a good reason before you can permit yourself to close out a profit.

B) *When in doubt, get out.* Don't gamble. Be sure, however, that your doubt is based on something real (fundamentals, market action, etc.), and not simply on your own nervousness about the price level. If it is only the price level that is making you nervous, then either stick with the winner or at worst use a more sensitive stop-loss point (like the six-day rule). Give the major trend all the chance you can to increase your profits.

C) *All major trends take a long time to work themselves out.* There are times when the best approach is just to sit and do nothing, letting the power of the underlying trend work for you while others argue about the day-to-day news. Be patient.

D) *Surprising price response to news is one of the most reliable price forecasters.* Bullish response to bear news, or vice-versa, means that the price had already discounted the news and the next move will probably go the other way. Actually, this is only one example of a wider principle: When a market doesn't do what it "should", then it will probably do what it "shouldn't", *and fairly soon.*

(Note that false breakouts, up or down, are also subsumed under this more general principle. When new lows are achieved in a long-term bear market, for example, the market "should" follow through with weakness—after all, it *is* a bear market. If, instead, it rallies quickly, this provides some evidence against the bear market premise).

E) *Volume, open interest, opinion indicators, etc., were not regarded by Mr. Hostetter as having much value.* Once in a while they may provide a little added confirmation to an opinion based on other considerations. However, they are not best evidence, and they sometimes serve more to confuse than to clarify.

F) Mr. Hostetter was a firm believer in *posting his own price charts daily.* This is a good part of where he derived his market "feel". All traders know that they sometimes get that strong feeling of near-certainty, which some attribute to intuition and which probably comes from a combination of signs whose significance has been learned and absorbed, yet never explicitly identified to oneself. The daily chart-posting provides an important input to this important sense. If one is going to listen to the news of the day, he should also pay attention to what the market heard and how it reacted. Eye and hand and pencil and paper make all this objective while providing a sensory input that helps it sink in. For example, if there is very bullish news and the market closes higher, this is usually sufficient to deter suspicion. However, what if the closing price failed to exceed the previous week's level, which had been attained under much less bullish circumstances? This *would* be suspicious, but the trader who hadn't posted his charts might have missed this subtle piece of feedback.

VII Summary

In this booklet I have done my best to describe the trading philosophy of a great speculator.

I knew Amos, I knew how generous he was with his ideas and his time, and I'm certain he would have wanted a booklet like this written. My hope is that I have been able to capture accurately the essentials of his trading philosophy and that this booklet will be of some value to others. I think Amos would have wished the same.

Until this point, I have focussed primarily on Mr. Hostetter's trading philosophy. I want to switch focus now and say something about Amos himself.

Although I did not have a long-standing friendship with Amos, I did meet and speak with him often enough during the past four years to form my own opinions about him. He was an inspiration to me, as a trader and as a man.

The mere fact of Amos' phenomenal success as a trader already says a great deal about him. It has long been my contention that the virtues required to make a good trader are to a large degree the same virtues that make a good man. Intelligence alone is not sufficient. Virtues of character are required. Amos' steady devotion to facts, facts, facts made him a man who had no choice but to be honest and sincere, always. He was a proud man, as he had every right to be, but he was quietly proud. I think he knew himself well enough to appreciate recognition from others, but not to need it.

He was a rational and benevolént man with an ever active and eager mind, still capable of being excited by ideas until the day of his death. He had strong opinions, but was never opinionated. He was disci-plined, but this discipline was of his own choosing, not forced by will power. He was a man who kept perspective, who rarely lost sight of the object he was headed toward.

Amos always did what he judged to be right, trusting in his own judgment and trusting in the operation of logic or justice to bring the appropriate reward.

SOME OBSERVATIONS ON TRADING IN COMMODITY FUTURES

One might assume that profitable commodity trading is a function of being right something over half the time. Starting with a correct idea is, of course, an important first step, but the next one is the more difficult; namely, converting this idea into a credit on the brokerage statement. This is where most failures occur. It is a source of amazement to me how many traders start with a correct idea, and end up with no profit, even though the move occurs just as expected. They are, of course, violating some basic trading rules, which are rather generally known, but not properly applied.

To force the application of sound trading principles to a commodity position, I have prepared a questionnaire to be answered before taking a position and before closing it out once the position is taken.

Questions to Answer Before Taking a Commodity Position

1. Do you think that a major trend has either started or is about to start in the commodity in question?

2. Is the contemplated trade in the direction of this trend?

3. Do you think that the move will be a substantial one (at least 10% of current price) and run for a considerable period of time (3 to 9 months)?

4. Have you selected an actual or approximate stop loss point where you would be willing to admit you are wrong and take your loss?

(At this point summarize your ideas as follows: I believe that ___________________________ now selling at ___________
          commodity and contract month   current price
will advance to _________ in _________ months. Meanwhile,
    decline
I will stop my position at ___________. Now proceed with the questionaire.)

5. Is the potential move that you visualize at least twice the loss you will take if stopped out?

6. Is the loss that you will take if stopped out (on the number of contracts being considered) less than 25% of the equity in the commodity account?

-2-

If the anser to all these questions is yes, then make the trade. One negative answer kills it.

Questions to Answer Before Closing a Commodity Position
(Assuming the stop order has not been executed)

1. Does the position show a loss?

2. Has it reached the price objective which you expected when the trade was initiated?

3. Have you held it for the period of time stated above?

4. Are you convinced that the major trend has changed since your forecast?

If all answers are "no", you must hold your position; if the answer to any one question is "yes", you may close the trade, but you are not compelled to do so.

Now for a few comments on the rationale behind these questions. If you are after excitement, jump in and out as often as you wish. But, I am assuming your motive is profit. If so, you should play only when major trends exist and only in the direction of the trend. Never go short to catch a dip in a bull market or buy for a rally in a bear market. Never trade in a "trading market". Leave a market strictly alone until you feel there is a trend going - then play the trend and, what is very hard to do, stay with it! Don't grab a quick profit. Once a position moves in your favor, sit stubbornly until you think the entire trend has run its course. Don't form opinions as to intermediate moves. In fact, don't even watch it too closely. Just hold on. If the 4 point profit shrinks to a 2 point profit, don't panic. Save your fears and panic for the position that started off with a 2 cent loss. On that one, jump out as quickly as you'd like - the sooner the better.

Commodities are fast moving markets with low margins. Hence, you must decide in advance at what point you will limit you loss and stick to your decision. Also this "exposure" on any given trade should not exceed one quarter of the equity in your account. Should a loss equal as much as one half of your equity, it is obvious that two losses in a row will put you out of business.

On closing out a trade, you will note that our rules say you "may" act under certain conditions. For instance, your price objective may be reached but not your time objectives. If you wish to hold

longer well and good. A position that is going with you tends to
keep going with you and your initial estimate of the move may have
been conservative. A loss by overstaying a market is not one of the
common mistakes. In fact, holding a profitable position a little
longer will win far more often that it will lose. The big risk is
closing a good position too soon. Hence, the close-out questions
are geared to locking you into a position for a substantial profit
or until proved wrong.

ABHostetter
4-15-66

Author's Note: Mr. Hostetter often placed even stricter demands upon himself than the above requires. He usually demanded a risk:reward ratio of better than 1:2, which is the minimum implied by question five. Also, as is noted under *Money Management* in the body of the text, he almost never risked as much as 25 percent of his equity on one idea, which is the maximum permitted by question six.

58

This appendix consists of a list of observations, cautions, market maxims, and general advice to the trader. All are *verbatim* from Mr. Hostetter's own writing, with the following exceptions:

Some of the original observations used stocks instead of commodities, although the essential principle applied to both. In these instances, I have replaced the reference to the stock market with a general reference to markets, and marked the change with parentheses.

Parentheses also mark the minor grammatical or typographical corrections made to a few of the original statements.

THE DANGERS IN TRADING CAUSED BY HUMAN NATURE

1. Fear—fearful of profit and one acts too soon.
2. Hope—hope for a change [in the] forces against one.
3. Lack of confidence in one's own judgment.
4. Never cease to do your own thinking.
5. A man must not swear eternal allegiance to either the bear or bull side. His concern lies in being right.
6. Laziness prevents a trader from keeping posted to the minute.
7. The individual fails to stick to *facts*.
8. People believe what it pleases them to believe.

DON'TS

1. Don't sacrifice your position for fluctuations.
2. Don't expect the market to end in a blaze of glory. Look out for *warnings*.
3. Don't expect the tape to be a lecturer. It's enough to see that something is wrong.

4. Never try to sell at the top. It isn't wise. Sell after a reaction if there is no rally.
5. Don't imagine that a [market] that has once sold at 150 must be cheap at 130.
6. Don't buck the market trend.
7. Don't look for breaks. Look out for warnings.
8. Don't try to make an average from a losing game.
9. Never keep goods that show a loss and sell those that show a profit. Get out with the least loss and sit tight for greater profits.

SUGGESTIONS

1. Experience must teach. Follow it invariably.
2. Observation gives the best tips of all. Observe [market] behavior and experience shows how to profit.
3. Buying on a rising market is the comfortable way. The point is not so much to buy as cheap as possible or go short at top prices, but to buy and sell at the right time.
4. Remember [a market is] never too high for you to begin buying or too low to begin selling. Let your tape reading show you when to begin. After the initial transaction don't make a second unless the first shows a profit.
5. There is a great deal in starting right in every enterprise.
6. When something happens on which you did not count when your plans were made, it behooves you to utilize the opportunity.
7. In a bear market it is always wise to cover if complete demoralization develops suddenly.
8. Stick to facts only and govern your actions accordingly.
9. What is abnormal is seldom a desirable factor in a trader's calculations. If a [market] doesn't act right, don't touch it.